I0435694

Trout Country Wandering

Stories of Fishing and Nature

Joseph Friedrichs

Publisher's Note: This is a work of fiction. Names, characters and places are either the product of the author's imagination or are used fictitiously. Any resemblance to actual persons, business establishments or events is entirely coincidental.

Published by Fine Street Media
2900 11th Ave. South
Minneapolis, MN 55407

ISBN:-13:978-1499158052
ISBN-10: 149915805X

For every fish that got away.

CONTENTS

Brown Trout Blues

We grew up fishing the trout waters of North Iowa. For every turn in the narrow creeks that cut through seemingly endless cornfields, my friend John Carlson and I could point out two holes where trout were sure to be hiding. In other words, we knew the land, we knew the water and we knew where to catch fish. Not bad for a couple of otherwise rebellious teenagers.

One particular fishing spot we adored was the Blue Pit in Mason City, a speckle on the map not too far from the Minnesota border. The pit was an old rock quarry that had filled via a natural spring and decades of rainfall and snowmelt. The water was clear, damn clear, in fact. When fishing from the shoreline it was possible to see the bottom at depths of 15 feet. The waters were home to trout, mostly rainbows. The occasional lunker-brown trout could be seen swimming through the crystal waters, driving both men and boys mad. The browns were smart, elusive fish.

Being young and from Iowa, we grew up fishing with bobbers, sinkers and old fashioned rods and reels. Once you knew how to tie a hook to your line you were in the club. Simple as that. For bait we used night crawlers. We caught the large worms in our backyards at night using cheap flashlights and empty coffee cans half-full of dirt. It was a brilliant system: catch the worms, catch the fish, bring home dinner. Everybody wins. Well, perhaps not the fish.

John and I fished at the Blue Pit several times a week from the ages of 13 to 17. During the winter we fished on the north side of the pit, where trout gathered in large schools in the deeper water. During the summer we stood on the shore near an old chimney that had once been associated with the rock quarry. We figured it was the remnants of a tiny shack where the miners all drank beer and straight whiskey following a hard-day's work. We were wishful thinkers even at that age. You had to use your creative mind to enjoy growing up in Iowa. If you couldn't romanticize your existence, all you had left was corn and homework.

Summer fishing was the best at the Blue Pit. It is also where my heart was broken by a trophy-sized brown trout. It was the first fish to ever keep me up at night. The first to haunt my dreams. The brown trout taught me about loss.

The sun was preparing to set on another day in late August the day I was defeated by the big brown, or Trout Hunter, as we refer to the fish these days. The temperature was 60-degrees. The air was calm, with afternoon winds having gone to rest. Across the Blue Pit it was quiet, with only the slight ripples cast by thirsty insects. Occasionally, far from our outpost near the chimney, a trout would jump from the cool waters.

Although we had been fishing for several hours, our only catch of the day had been a small rainbow trout John had lucked into almost immediately upon our arrival. With an anticipation of great gangs of trout to be caught that evening, he causally tossed the small rainbow back to the clear waters of the pit.

"Going to be plenty of fish biting tonight," John said. "Best plan is to pace ourselves so we don't limit out too quickly."

Indeed.

Now that we hadn't encountered so much as a nibble from a fish since that first rainbow, our attitudes had shifted gears. We'd discussed our usual topics at length: girls, sports… and girls.

"She's going to call me tonight, I can feel it," John had a habit of saying about Heather Kohlers, a neighborhood girl he'd been badgering for years. Most often she would ignore my fishing friend until he was about to snap, only to revive his youthful desire when all appeared lost.

I was moments away from telling John the evening at the Blue Pit was a bust when my bobber began to do the famous jig it does when a trout is about to bite. The foam contraption slid slightly to the left, then went straight up again. Next it dipped and pulled again to the left. After that, it vanished.

"There it goes!" I exclaimed.

"Easy now," John said, "let him take it. This could be a big one. I don't see a school of fish around. It's a loner."

I allowed the fish to take the bait and swim deep into the pit. A slight breeze blew my brown hair from my forehead. At the same time, line escaped from the open bail of my reel with rapid succession. My heart thumped inside my chest. I could hear John speaking in the background, though what words he uttered I will never know. My world had become the fish. My very being extended from the fishing pole to the water.

With the grace of a deer and the swiftness of a farm cat, I set the hook. There are few feelings worse than a slack line after attempting to set the hook on a fish. This time, however, the line remained tight. Something was on the other end.

"Got him!" I yelled.

"What is it?" John demanded to know. "A nice one?"

From the weight I felt when the hook was set, I knew it was a monster. The fish thrashed and rolled in the depths to which it had ventured. We could see its golden body whirl from our spot on the shore. It was a brown trout. A trophy.

"Sweet Jesus," John muttered.

There is a dimension fishermen enter when they have a large catch on the line. It is an altered state of mind unlike anything produced by a chemical or any such mood-altering substance. The world shuts off around the fisherman during these rare and cherished episodes. When I set the hook that afternoon at the Blue Pit, I entered that zone.

"Get the net ready," I said.

John did as any good fishing companion would and crept toward the shoreline with our large net. He rolled up his sleeves and waited to fulfill his duty.

With precision and confidence, I battled the fish. It took several deep dives while I kept the line tight by resisting his efforts. It swam to the left, then out, away from the shore on which John and I stood. Had a marching band walked past at that very instant, I would not have noticed. Perhaps some miraculous, stunning-blonde beauty was walking along the shoreline near me. If she did, I never saw her. All I knew at that moment was the fish and the Blue Pit.

After yet another run in the opposite direction of the shore, the fish changed its plan of escape. It bolted toward the surface with the confidence and aggression of a young fighter in the ring. As the sun began to sink, the trout emerged. It shattered the calm of the pit and the evening. In all of its glory, the trout hung completely out of the water for a moment, seeming to dance on top of the Blue Pit. John and I stood motionless. Our mouths hung open like Neanderthals.

And then, without so much as looking in our direction, the fish shook the hook. It sprung from the trout's mouth like a dentist removing a tooth from some gassed-out patient. The fish was free. The water quickly went calm. The evening air grew still. John gasped for much-needed oxygen.

I went home that night and didn't mention the brown trout that got away. My mother knew something was up when I didn't reach for seconds on her famous green-bean casserole. I didn't bother to explain the aching in my heart. Nobody would understand, perhaps not even John. It was a 30-inch brown trout and it defeated me.

While tossing sleeplessly in bed that night, the notions that my hook was not sharp enough, or set properly, or any number of such plausible excuses swam through my mind. In the end, I was left with the brown trout blues. It settled in my soul and has never left. It was the fish of a lifetime and I missed that chance.

I live for another opportunity at his equal.

The Fire and the Bottle

It was a protest against love. The idea was to flee the city and head for the mountains. It was Valentine's Day and my friend Ryan and I were in no mood for buying flowers or chocolate hearts. The girls had been particularly vicious of late, so solitude and nature were in demand.

The previous evening, Feb. 13, 2004, Ryan had phoned me to explain his current romantic situations.

"I've got nothing going," he said. "Girls are driving me nuts. It is enough to make one want to tighten the old noose and go for that last great swing."

With a few other sentiments and expletives, he described how a blonde girl in his biology class at the University of Montana was "driving him out of his gourd." There was also a brunette in his environmental-studies class who made it impossible to think, both at home and during lecture hours.

"She sits near me and I spend the entire class thinking of something clever to say when we're dismissed," Ryan said. "And when we exit the building, I walk right past her without saying a damn word. It's all killing me."

My own romantic endeavors weren't faring much better. Within the past month, my heart had been trampled by approximately 25 girls. I was a fool when it came to women, and my track record proved it. Of the 25 aforementioned females, and I had managed to go on a date with only one. The others either turned me down flat or simply ignored my flirtations altogether. I was fool in the game. The only hairs found on my bed sheets were my own. And I hadn't washed the sheets in about six months.

Ryan picked me up at 10 a.m. on Valentine's Day morning. His green Toyota pickup truck bounced and roared up my steep driveway. It was obvious Ryan had a hangover. He wore dark sunglasses even though it was overcast. The darkness came as no surprise, as the Missoula Valley often spends its winters covered in a foggy haze of inversion.

"Women will be the death of me," Ryan said, his truck coming to a halt less than six inches from my shoeless toes. "Last night was terrible."

"I thought you were staying in last night?" I said. "You know, to study and get ready for this trip?"

"I was," Ryan said, "but then I wanted to go out for a beer. Next thing I know, I ended up taking shot after shot with some older woman. I paid the entire bar tab for us. It came to something like $75."

"Did you get any action?"

"She kissed me on the cheek and then said she had to

go throw up. By then it was bar time, 2 a.m. It was a nightmare."

"Let's get the hell out of Dodge," I said.

Ryan helped me load my oversized blue backpack into the open bed of his pickup. Inside the heavy pack were a yellow sleeping bag, an assortment of cooking supplies, two pairs of socks, a pair of mittens and a quart of bourbon.

"You get the booze?" Ryan asked.

"You know it, buddy," I said. "Your favorite, Ten High bourbon, plastic jug."

We escaped Missoula to the south on Highway 93. Near the town of Lolo we turned to the west and before long we were in Idaho. The remote Jerry Johnson Hot Springs were our destination. They are a beautiful, natural phenomenon located deep in the Clearwater National Forest. A half dozen hot-tub sized pools of warm water located along the banks of a beautiful mountain stream. It was the only place we could think of to escape the sentiments of a holiday we wanted no part of. Or, perhaps, it wanted nothing to do with us. Either way, the warm waters of the naturally-heated pools and the surrounding pine and cedar trees were calling.

"When was the last time you were up to the springs?" I asked Ryan, mostly checking to make sure he was still awake behind the wheel.

"Jolene and I came up here sometime last fall," Ryan said. "We argued the whole way home."

"How the heck can you find something to argue about in this beautiful place?" I asked, staring out my passenger-side window at the majestic surroundings. Snow-covered peaks loomed in every direction. Creeks, rivers and canyons seemed to be around every turn of the winding mountain road.

"I don't know what we argued about," Ryan said. "We always found something. If she wanted sausage, I wanted pepperoni. If she wanted cheeseburgers, I wanted tacos."

Somehow, I knew exactly what he meant.

About 2 hours after we left Missoula, Ryan and I arrived to the parking area and trailhead leading to the hot springs. Without much conversation, we tightened the laces of our boots, put on our winter-hiking gear and strapped on our heavy backpacks. Just after noon, we charged across the large wooden bridge leading from the highway to the forest. It began to snow.

"Right about now," Ryan said. "That old lady from the bar last night is waking up in a puddle of her own puke."

It was a terrible thought. It was time for the woods to heal our bodies and our minds.

The walk from the trailhead to the springs – even during the winter – is a pleasant, enchanting stroll. Large trees stand on either side of the trail, the creek rustling not far below. Animals, including moose, elk, mountain lion and wolves follow the same trail, hoping to find an easy meal in the otherwise tough winter months. Wolves, as Ryan and I were soon to discover, were common along the trail.

About an hour into our hike, we arrived to the hot springs. The smell of sulfur hung heavy in the cold air. Steam rose from the warm pools and green moss grew nearby, marking the frozen perimeter where the geothermal activity ceased. There was not a human in sight. It was perfect.

"Peace at last!" Ryan yelled. "Thank God almighty, we have peace at last!"

According to Forest Service regulations, campers are not allowed to set up shop within one mile of the hot springs. Too many degenerates would ruin the land, we reasoned. Therefore, Ryan and I had no issues with having to hike beyond the springs to establish our camp. This also meant we would have to hike a mile back to the springs, and another mile back to camp later that night.

"We've got time," I said. "Let's keep moving and set up and get a fire going. We'll soak later."

Ryan agreed without saying a word. He pressed onward through the forest. The trail beyond the hot springs was far less traveled. Someone wearing snowshoes, likely a forest ranger, had hiked the trail. Based on the faintness of the tracks, the person had likely been here several weeks before. Also decorating the trail were dozens of deer, elk and rabbit tracks.

"Lots of food up here for somebody," Ryan said. "Or, something."

We both laughed, knowing there were plenty of hungry carnivores in the area. We were both experienced hikers in the wilds of the West, so our progress was not hindered by fear.

After another hour of hiking, Ryan and I came to a perfect campsite located along the banks of Warm Springs Creek. The terrain was flat. There was more than enough room for our tent and to have a large fire. I started to work on setting up the tent. Ryan went off to gather firewood. We both took a swig of bourbon.

"Hot damn," Ryan said, shaking his head from the strong taste of alcohol.

Before long, Ryan and I had a camp established. Our tent was secure. Sleeping bags were rolled out in anticipation of our arrival later that evening. Ryan had the fire going and a surplus of wood to burn sat nearby. It was time to drink.

"You know," Ryan said as he poured several ounces of bourbon into a small-plastic cup, "the thing is, when I'm out here I couldn't care less about getting a girl's phone number. I just want to stay alive. In the city, I go nuts thinking about women."

"That's why we're here, my friend," I said. "Escaping without having to destroy ourselves."

We both laughed and took another gulp of booze.

Just before dark, Ryan and I decided it was time to march back to the hot springs and take a soak. Our alcohol-buzz was steady but not overpowering. Our minds were limber, our moods jolly.

"Think of all those poor suckers getting dressed up right now," John exclaimed. "All those dinner reservations and flowers that'll be dead in a week. And here we are, with the moon and the wild things of this planet. This is living!"

Indeed.

And so we set forth with thoughts of warm waters on our minds. We walked with an easy pace, singing strange songs and laughing. Ryan was in front, with me close behind.

"All you need is love," I sang, doing my best to honor the Beatles' classic tune.

About halfway to the springs, Ryan came to a sudden and dramatic halt.

"Blood," he said. "Fresh."

I peaked around his lengthy frame. Sure enough, red

stains littered the white snow. Chunks of fur clung to the crisp edge of the icy trail. A rabbit had been slaughtered, no question.

"Wolves?" I asked.

Ryan, who grew up in the northern woods of Montana, was an experienced hunter with excellent tracking skills.

"Sure as shit," he said.

We both crouched near the scene of the killing. The area was trampled by animal activity. Large-paw prints were everywhere.

"This happened within the past 20 minutes," Ryan said. "This blood is barely iced over. It's not warm, but it's not completely frozen."

The hair stood up on the back of my neck. Whatever had butchered this rabbit was likely still nearby. A strange silence gripped the chilled air.

"I knew I should have brought my pistol," Ryan calmly stated.

We never made it to the hot springs that night. After coming across the bloody scene in the forest, our only comforts were the fire and the bottle. It was a cold night in a dark forest. The wolves were feeding. That much was certain.

"You know," Ryan said later that evening while we sat around our large fire, "those wolves ripped that rabbit to pieces. They destroyed it."

He lifted the bottle and took a huge gulp. His eyes were serious and his voice was firm.

"They ripped its heart out," he said. "It was a Valentine's Day massacre. There was no mercy."

After an awkward moment of silence, he continued.

"That would have been me, had I stayed in town tonight. It would have been a bloodbath, my friend. I would be the rabbit, and the women of Missoula would be the wolves."

We lifted our glasses to the air and roared with laughter. The fire burned a good-clean burn. The moon lit the sky with an iridescent hue.

It was the single greatest moment of my life.

Steps to Nature

It was the first day of summer vacation and my recently-divorced father came charging into the bedroom my brother and I still shared at the age of 13. He had a list in his hand and I knew we were doomed. My father is a man who finds inspirations in scripted adventures. He rarely conjures the ideas himself, relying on travel magazines and brochures to do his thinking and planning.

"I've got it, kids!" he exclaimed. "Eight brilliant ideas to get us outside this summer and have some fun doing it. Fresh air, hearty exercise, beautiful landscapes, wildlife encounters... just imagine!"

He found the list in some family magazine that is no longer in print. With a list as deadening as the one my father found, I understand why the magazine failed.

I will now describe the eight ideas from the magazine and tell what happened to us that summer as we followed the list. Just know that it changed my life, and it's true that the sun still rises even when you're going through hell.

1- Sleep in the backyard: First off, at the time we attempted this, my family lived in the heart of Kansas City. Our backyard was 80 percent gravel and 20 percent wasteland. There was neither a fence to enclose us, nor one to provide us with a sense of security.

"You don't need a pile of equipment to spend your first night under the stars. Choose a beautiful summer evening and take your sleeping bags outside in your yard," the magazine read.

Well, for our first adventure, my dad tried to set up the tent in the wasteland area, only to watch it blow away and down the alley before nightfall. My brother heard a gunshot at 9 p.m. and we all went inside shortly thereafter. Our summer adventures were just beginning!

2- Find a family-friendly campground: After accepting our backyard was no place for camping, my dad drove us to Jackson County's Longview Lake. The idea was to try car-camping in a scenic, natural area. My dad was glowingly optimistic while driving to the lake. My brother and I slept most of the way.

The campground was nearly full when we got there, but at least we had a platform for our new tent. We also had a campfire pit and a new grill.

"Let's set up camp, take a walk, cook dinner, sing songs, and then curl up in our tents for a cozy family sleep," my dad said.

Not long after this beautiful proclamation, it started to rain. And rain it did. The merciless skies dropped more than 3-inches of water in about 90 minutes. We sat in the car and listened to "A Prairie Home Companion" on public radio. It was the first time I remember contemplating suicide.

3- Try canoe camping: This is the point during the summer when I realized my father had gone mad. The man worked as a male nurse and had never once paddled a canoe. What convinced him that spending hundreds of dollars renting waterproof equipment bags and other camping gear along with a large canoe was a good idea is so far beyond me that neither science nor religion can provide comforting answers.

"The river is wide, deep, and fast, so the water does most of the work," my father said as we pushed off onto the Missouri River, heading west.

Within an hour of us leaving the small marina, our canoe became stuck in a vicious eddy. We sat there spinning in the backwaters for more than three hours, unable to budge. Other canoeists and boaters mocked us repeatedly, none of them offering to help. Angry and hostile, we finally escaped from the eddy and pulled ashore. My father used his cell phone to have the outfitting company come pick us up.

"Next time, you'll be pros!" the guy at the canoe-rental office said when we were leaving.

Without my father knowing, I flipped the man the middle finger.

4- Hike to a hut: This was supposed to be Dad's fail-proof plan. Apparently tucked into the woods of Missouri there are tiny huts people can rent for a sort of glorified camping experience.

"They're a great way to introduce your kids to backpacking without having to haul quite so much gear. You'll have a solid roof over your heads in case of bad weather," the magazine read.

Out hut was located inside the boundaries of Watkins Mill State Park. I have to give Dad some credit here; he had the right idea. All the camping and cooking gear was waiting for us inside the hut, also known as a yurt. We only had to hike .75 miles to get there from a paved parking lot. I have to admit, even my brother had a spring in his step that day.

Well, when we got there the hut was infested with mice and insects, namely spiders. We hiked back to our car in silence and my father called the park office demanding a refund. It was the first time I heard my father curse.

We spent the night at a Holiday Inn watching old Chevy Chase movies. It was a marathon on TNT to celebrate the actor's many comedic accomplishments.

Only my father found the films amusing.

5- Focus on the fun in nature: The idea here was to turn the dial down a notch. There were to be no overnight debacles. No canoe rentals. The magazine said it was awesome to spend an afternoon outdoors while walking down a trail. It was really that easy: walking for fun.

"Hike at a reasonable pace," my dad instructed us. "Take frequent breaks for water and snacks. Enjoy yourselves!"

His tone was becoming more desperate with each failed experiment in the great outdoors. The magazine suggested we sing songs while we hiked to help add color to our experience. My dad sang one verse of "99 Bottles of Beer" before his voice faded out to a quiet whistle and eventually silence resumed. Not long after that, my brother was stung by a wasp and we went home.

6- Join an organized backpacking trip: Having failed alone, Dad turned to professional leaders who could teach us how to set up camp, cook meals, store our food, read topographic maps and administer first aid.

"Best of all," said Alex, our backpacking guide, "you and your kids will explore the incredible beauty and biodiversity of a real wilderness area in the company of other fun adults and kids."

It was late July and Dad was getting desperate. We drove to Denver and met Alex and others who would join us for a backpacking trip into the Rocky Mountains.

Well, it turns out Alex was a con artist with a deep history of theft and deceit. After handing over $600 cash, Alex said he would lead us all to a trailhead about 30-miles west of Denver. Instead, Alex ran a red light at a busy intersection, ditching us and the other families. No one in the group ever saw him again. We reported the crime to local authorities and went back to Kansas City.

7- Take a real backpacking trip: Having purchased the gear we needed, dad refused to give up and planned his own multi-day backpacking trip in Arkansas's Ozark Mountains. He purchased topographical maps of the area where we planned to hike. We all pitched in ideas and planned a menu for our scheduled two-night stay in the Ozark backcountry. Dad plunked down $300 for a digital camera "to help us remember what is bound to be an incredible trip."

Things were all going according to plan until dad got a call from his sister, my aunt. It turns out my father had been adopted and never been told. His sister discovered the news while sorting through old documents belonging to my now-deceased grandparents.

We went home and dad got drunk for a week straight.

8- Camp at camp: In this last-stitch effort to get us outdoors, Dad sent us away for the final week of summer. The magazine said summer camps were "great places to meet other children who enjoy the outdoors."

By this point, my brother and I loathed Mother Nature so much that all we desired were video games, a flat-screen television and endless bowls of ice cream.

Anyhow, at the camp I got bit by a tick and came home with a mysterious infection.

School started just after Labor Day and the thought of spending another minute in the "great outdoors" makes me whimper like a timid mouse.

I understand why the magazine where dad found the list is no longer publishing. It ruined my summer. I shall feel like the bastard son of Mother Nature…forever.

Brush Bears

April finally brought a much-needed spring. The seemingly endless winter in Oregon had been brutal. Throughout the previous five months, whatever snow had fallen in the Cascade Mountains was more slush than powder. The woods were heavy with the glue-like substance. Trees everywhere slouched over, their limbs hanging like the arms of tired old men.

I'd spent most of my winter delivering wood to wealthy homeowners. It was a meager living, but I was proud to be my own boss. I had no co-workers. It was my own operation. I harvested the timber. I split the logs. I delivered the wood. Life was good and I worked when the demand was there, not when someone told me to. That was always the problem with a job: other people.

The town where I live is a beautiful little community known as Ashland, Oregon. Some folks say it is overrun with hippies and transplants from the San Francisco Bay Area. I am neither a hippie nor from California. It comes with pride that I call myself an Oregonian. These are my woods. This snow, this damned slush blanketing the forests, it's my snow, for better or worse.

And until the bear came, I'd never realized just how

powerful the expansive forest I call a backyard truly is.

William Shakespeare made famous the phrase, "Beware the Ides of March." In his play, *Julius Caesar*, a soothsayer tells Caesar that the Ides, or middle of March, will bring terrible news. Unfortunately for Caesar, this foreboding meant death. For me, after such a brutal winter, the Ides meant losing a delicious dinner of fresh rainbow trout because of some crazed black bear.

How this bear came to cross my life's path is a matter of pure circumstance. For the record, black bears are the most common and widely-distributed bears in North America. I've seen hundreds of them in my life, right here in Oregon. They're interesting creatures, but, honestly, I could take them or leave them. I get more thrills from catching a huge steelhead than I do from seeing some manic bear barreling down the trail. Heck, bears stink worse than the rotten entrails they usually eat from the chest cavity of some poor elk or deer. Fish are what make Oregon so unique. Bears are just sort of… around.

So, as I was saying, the bear that changed my life came to me as a matter of circumstance. There I was, enjoying the spring weather and going for my limit of rainbow trout. I was fishing a remote section of the Rogue River, when the beast appeared. He looked haggard and disheveled. His eyes were dark. All of his hair was matted and greasy. Quite frankly, his appearance reminded me of what I looked like every morning during my drinking days. I haven't looked like that in nearly three years, I remember thinking as the bear approached my stringer of recently-caught trout.

Okay, let me point out one fact: I'm all about sharing. When it comes to helping people in need, I have no problem stepping up to the plate. You know those penny trays at a gas station where you can leave loose change to help out the next guy in line? Well, I've been known to leave quarters in those trays. That's the kind of guy I am.

It's just that when it comes to bears, I'm not the giving type. They have their side of the creek, and I'll be dammed if I don't have mine. So when this greasy son-of-a-gun came up to my fishing hole and starting snorting and sniffing all around, I knew there was going to be trouble.

I had two beautiful rainbows on my stringer, the result of my excellent casting and bouncing of a baetis-mayfly nymph all morning. The trout were timid, but they could be caught with the right kind of precision and patience. My dedication had paid off. For the record, both of the fish I landed were about 18 inches in length.

While taking a break from the fishing, I climbed a small bluff overlooking the river. My loving wife had packed me a homemade meatloaf sandwich for lunch. She wasn't much of a cook, but I loved her all the same.

"You can't have everything in this life," my dad was fond of saying. "But if you play your cards right, you can get it steady and not spend all your money chasing loose tail."

Indeed, Pa.

I was about three-quarters finished with my sandwich when the bear first appeared. He came out of the thick brush as though he'd been spying on me all morning. Some kind of brush bear, I figured. Brush bears are those that linger in bogs and marshlands. They keep hidden nearly all the time except for two things: eating and procreating.

I smelled him first, I suppose. It was that potent combination of sweat and dirt. Of dried blood and rain. Man did that bear stink!

So there he came, wandering out of the thicket. Though he was pretending to be sniffing about and confused by the whole scene, I knew he was on a mission. His nose was zeroed- in on my trout. And there they sat, carelessly floating in the shallows of an eddy, about 10-inches from shore.

I watched the bear from my post on the bluff. He knew I was watching, no doubt about it. And still, as though he owned the entire state of Oregon, the bear strolled over to my fish. It had been several hours since I landed both of the trout, and yet they clung to some semblance of life. They had no chance of survival, but they weren't entirely stiff and dead quite yet. And more importantly, they were to be dinner for my wife and me that very night. Nothing tastes better than fresh trout pulled from cold water. I knew that, and so did the damn bear.

When he finally reached my fish, the bear turned one last time in my direction. I swear to this day he was smiling. A sheepish grin on his face told me of his plan. And sure enough, in one smooth motion of his left paw, he ripped one of the trout right off the metal stringer. The fish casually spun in the water for a brief moment. Then the bear dunked its head into the river and grabbed the trout. With a devilish look, the bear turned and started ruthlessly eating the fish.

"Hey!" I yelled. "What the hell is this?!"

Without so much as a twitch, the bear swallowed what remained of the first fish and turned for the other.

"That's my dinner!" I shouted.

I stood up to, well, I don't really know what my intentions were. I had to do something, or at least felt I had to do something. There was a bear eating my dinner. I spent all morning catching those fish. I'd been cheated. It was man versus beast and I appeared to be on the losing end.

"Get outta here!" I said confidently. "Get! Get!"

The bear, staring in my direction, continued to mash my trout between its sharp incisors. It swallowed, moved from the water back to the dry bank and continued to stare at me.

There are moments in life when a sense of serenity delivers the message of our purpose on this planet. Likewise, there are moments of supreme terror that make our lives seem pointless and too fast to understand. What happened next made me realize how little power I truly have here on Earth.

"That was my dinner!" I yelled at the bear.

This final insult pushed the bear over the edge. With confidence and grace, he stood on his hind legs. From resembling a greasy cow one moment, the bear suddenly transformed into a tower of power and aggression. It opened its mouth, revealing a locker of sharp teeth. Shards of trout flesh and guts clung to the edges of the bear's mouth.

And then the animal roared.

I've run reasonably fast several times in my life. One Halloween a crazed farmer chased my friend and me off his property near Medford because we were fixing to steal some pumpkins off his land. Another time I had to outrun some jerk up in Portland who was trying to steal my cab at the airport. Though never in my life have I moved faster than when that bear roared on the banks of the Rogue River.

The recent snowmelt left giant puddles all over the trail leading from the river to the lot where my pickup was parked. Some were nearly a foot deep. It didn't matter. I hauled through them like a semi roaring down the interstate. I never looked back. Fortunately, I had my $400 fly rod at my side when I sat down to eat the sandwich from my loving wife. I was able to pick up the rod, my tackle and my lucky fishing hat before bolting from the bluff. All I left behind was the stringer that once held my beautiful trout.

The black bear probably spent a good portion of his morning watching me fish. When I took a lunch break, he came out to steal my fish. It's as simple as that. I challenged the beast and came away with a heart full of fear.

I am not a vengeful man. I do not pray for misfortune to fall upon anybody or anything.

All I have to say to the brush bear is this: come hunting season, I know where you live.

The German

Nothing changes, it only seems to.

The German man from youth taught me that. He spoke those words to me on a cold day in October. The German taught me much about life. Mostly, he taught me about fishing.

At the age of 14, I am ashamed to admit, I still didn't know how to clean a fish. I understood the basic concept: use a knife to cut away the meat. It was the process I didn't understand. Like, where did you insert the blade? What did you do with the head? How do you get rid of all those bones?

It was the white-haired German who taught me. Like I said, it was this good fellow who taught me damn near everything I know about fishing. Everything artistic, anyhow.

"When it comes to trout, the art is in patience and how you present the bait," he said. "Now when it comes to cleaning trout, there is no art. You skin the bastards."

The German was a blunt individual.

When you break it down to its simplest form, fishing is nothing more than a form of deceit. A fish thinks it is going to be fed, only to wind up with a sharp hook in its mouth. And in this fashion the deceitful prosper.

However, there is more to fishing though than simply

casting a line and hoping for the best. One must deal with variables such as weather, seasons, time of day, as well as water clarity and depth. Your surroundings play a very important role and change every day, often every hour when it comes to fishing. The German taught me this.

A little background on the German: He was born August 27, 1912, in Andernach, Germany. His father taught mathematics and his mother worked in a small bakery. At the age of 19, the German left his homeland. After his departure, the German never spoke to his mother or father again.

The German arrived in New York City on September 25, 1931. He worked in a deli for seven months before catching a bus to Clear Lake, Iowa. The German has lived there, working as a plumber and driving a large blue van ever since.

I first met the German in the summer of 1995. He was 83 years old and I was a teenager. His hair was ghostly white. Mine was brown. He stood just over 6-feet tall. I was a foot shorter. The only thing we had in common was that we both liked to fish. And fish we did.

"You ignorant boy," the German said to me one afternoon, his accent still thick and powerful. "You don't cast into the shallows. You go deep, out there."

The German pointed the index finger on his right hand out toward the middle of the pond where we fished.

That was my introduction to the German. Without acknowledging what he said, I recast my line into the deeper water. Within 30 seconds, I had a trout on the line. After landing the fish I looked in the German's direction. He was smoking a hand-rolled cigarette and smiling.

After that, I began to fish near the German every afternoon when I visited the pond where we both partook in our favorite pastime. He didn't seem to mind my presence, though we rarely spoke.

On the afternoon of October 15, 1996, however, things changed between the German and me.

It was a terrible day on all fronts. I failed a math test that day during school. The temperature was 40 degree. A fierce wind blew in cold from the north. Winter was around the corner, and the open-water fishing season on the pond was soon to end. The German knew it. I knew it. That is why we were the only diehards fishing that afternoon.

And despite our efforts, we had collected not a single strike from below the surface. I should mention that the German was a tactical man in all his fishing endeavors. I've come to the pond to find him fly fishing from a scraggily boulder 15-feet out from the bank. I've also found him in the far corners of the pond, bushwhacking through terrible thicket with a worm and a bobber as his means of catching a trout.

In the fall, however, we always used a minnow for bait. It worked best to fish the minnow deep, dangled about five-feet below a plastic bobber. Two split-shot sinkers were essential for keeping the minnow down and for providing extended casting ability. The German taught me this.

Neither of us had any action with the fish during the first two hours on this particular day in October. As I said, not a strike. The waters were choppy and it appeared nothing would happen other than coming home cold and somewhat disgruntled.

And just like that, my bobber vanished.

And then the German's went down.

There are times in a fisherman's life when the stars align and good fortune comes to him. This was that day for the German. Likewise, it was that day for me. Following two hours of drudgery, the ensuing 20 minutes were a blur of fishing bliss and madness. After we landed our first two fish with success, both of them rainbows measuring 15 inches, we hooked new minnows to our lines and went back for more.

"They out there, boy," the German barked. "Get 'zem."

Indeed we did.

Before my line could properly descend on that follow-up cast to the first fish, the bobber was yanked under again. It shot down as though it were tied to a piano. I set the hook and the battle with trout number two started. A glance in the German's direction, and I saw that he too was fighting another fish.

This process, baiting the hook, casting out and reeling in a trout continued for the next 15 minutes without interruption. We each had our limit of trout at the end of it.

Without noticing, it had started to rain. The wind had picked up. The weather was absolutely terrible. My clothes were soaked in a Pacific-Coast kind of way. I hadn't prepared for the elements. I had neither raingear nor so much as a hat. It didn't matter though. We had our fish.

Standing there, near enough to the German to hear him quietly chuckling as we gutted and skinned our trout, I knew the day was ours. The rest of town was miserable. They were driving home from work, or class, or grocery shopping, or wherever they were coming from while the rain came down. The wind whipped their faces and vehicles and a general sadness came over them. The German and I felt the same wind that day and didn't pay it a lick of attention. Our victory was in our hands.

The German taught me about battling the elements, waiting for the prize. Nothing comes easy, and nothing changes. It takes patience in life. Good things will come.

The German taught me that.

Pheasant Hunters

There wasn't much pleasure in shooting my first pheasant. There wasn't for me, anyhow. I was 12 years old and hated waking up early on Saturday. My dad found some cheap thrill in rousing his children early on the weekends.

"Get up, boy," he would say loudly at my bedroom door.

After I woke up, it was always cold. It was cold inside our brick house. It was even colder outside. Hunting season for pheasants always started in the late fall. While other kids enjoyed Saturday morning cartoons or got to watch college football, I loaded a gun and went out to kill birds.

For my father, hunting was pure entertainment. It showed the power scale between man and bird. To me, it was drudgery. And this so-called "hunting" was nothing more than wandering through a godforsaken cornfield while the men drank beer and hoped for the pheasants to jump from their hiding spots. Then we shot them.

I remember the day I shot my first pheasant. To the east of me was a cow pasture. I was walking in thick grass inside a wooden fence. My dad was blocking at the other end. This meant he would try to keep pheasants from completely running away from the people walking through the field who were equipped with guns in their hands.

We got to about the middle of the field and I heard my dad yell something at me. I did not hear him until he said it a second time. He was trying to tell me that there had been a rooster that had run into the field directly in front of me. It took me a while to spot it, and when I finally did it would not fly up. I did not want to shoot at the ground because there were dogs around. I kicked at the pheasant and it flew up toward the pasture. I took a shot, and it fell to the ground with one shot. However, the bird was not yet dead. After our Spaniel retrieved the bird, it was still flapping and twitching. My dad yelled out for me to break the pheasant's neck. When our dog dropped the bird at my feet, I picked it up and wrung its neck as though it were a wet towel.

I was not very excited, first of all because my dad was already drinking beer heavily that day, and second of all because it was the first time I had killed something with a pulse. I didn't like when my dad and his friends drank so much beer. Anyhow, we took a few pictures and headed back to the farm.

I was told to clean all the pheasants we'd killed that morning, which totaled nine birds, including mine.

"I don't know how to clean the birds," I told my now-drunk dad.

Opening a fresh can of Old Milwaukee, he belched before he told me to pluck the back end of the bird first.

"Using them shears, boy," he said. "Snip through the skin of the abdomen and all the way around, and cut off the rear copula' inches of bird."

I stood there motionless like a prisoner taking orders.

"Then roll the bird over until his back is up," my dad continued. "Insert them shears and split the back all the way up to the neck. Pull the guts out the back and hose it out. Got it, boy?"

In reality, I had no choice.

That night we went to some hole known as Jacki's Café. I ordered a homemade cheese pizza. It was dreadful. The crust tasted like cardboard and the cheese was government issued. From the time we arrived until the time we left there was a constant traffic of other pheasant hunters. All of them appeared to be drunk on beer. When we were done, we went to get ice to store the pheasants in. We got back to the farm, and all the adults passed out.

I went outside to get my book and saw a large skunk. I came in and woke my dad, telling him there was a skunk. I was hesitant to go back, but my dad drug me outside. The coyotes were howling outside in all directions. I only got a glimpse of the skunk and was anxious to go back inside. My dad killed it with his shotgun.

My dad doesn't really remember my first pheasant-hunting experience. He is a blackout drinker with little concern for much else. I was forced to go hunting with him and his moronic buddies until I turned 18.

On that day, my 18th birthday, I moved away from the open pastures to the bright lights of New York City. The only grim connection to my childhood is that I work in a 5-star restaurant where pheasant is occasionally the main course special.

"If you ever need any help cleaning and gutting those birds," I told my first boss, "I can probably lend a hand."

Oregon Locomotion

My friends and family told me that hitchhiking was for crazy people. A morbid mode of transportation reserved only for those with no gleaming sense of reality. Hell, they said, if you go hitchhiking, you're going to die.

None of what they told me meant much. I listened. I considered. And I opted to hitchhike to Oregon's 7th highest peak in the Cascades – Mt. Thielsen.

Why not? I certainly had plenty of time to take on such a mission. No children. No pets. No moral sense of obligation. So I loaded my pack with enough food for three days, a sleeping bag, tent, reading material, a bottle of cheap red wine. And I hit the road.

The mighty mountain peak that is Mt. Thielsen is nestled just north of Crater Lake National Park, roughly 100 miles south of Bend. It's a jagged peak, often referred to as the Matterhorn of the Cascade Mountains. Until last week I'd only gazed at its stony, spindly peak from Highway 138 on my way west to the valley or coast. Thielsen was a legend. A myth. Not something that could actually be hiked upon.

I quit paying my car insurance the first week of June. There's no serious motive for choosing to do so, other than the fact I'd all but given up driving my vehicle. It's been sitting out in front of the house for going on two weeks without having been started, let alone moved. Biking and walking had taken over as my main methods of locomotion. Without a legal means to travel south to Thielsen, hitching seemed to be the most logical option.

I left Bend on a Tuesday. Although it was only 7:30 a.m. when I reached Highway 97, it was already snug outside. Not sweaty and scorching warm, just pleasant. I was wearing my trusty pair of well-worn Merrell boots/shoes, olive green hiking pants and a gray t-shirt with the script: "Brookings, A Quaint Little Drinking Town With A Fishing Problem." I held a stale cardboard sign made from a Pizza Mondo box that was nailed to a slender two-foot piece of wood. One side read "Crater Lake" and on the flip side was written "Bend" in large, darkly-stained letters.

Three minutes passed before I caught my first ride. It was a Mexican man who was going to work at the fire station in nearby Sunriver, a mere 8- miles south. Whatever, I thought of the quick ride, got to get this journey started somehow. So without hesitation I hopped in the cluttered van and the expedition was underway.

It never occurred to me that hitchhiking was unusual or dangerous. After all, it is simply standing along the road with your thumb out as you hope someone gives you a ride somewhere. Nothing more. Certainly nothing less. I'd hitchhiked once before. It was after the 2006 Bonnaroo Music Festival in Southern Tennessee. It was imperative I make it back to Raleigh, North Carolina in time to catch a flight the day after the festival came to an end. One option was to spend 30 hours taking the Greyhound bus. The other was to hitch. Fearing the wrath of ignorant scum crammed on a stank bus, I opted to stick out the thumb and test the odds. Twenty yards from the festival gate, two girls, who happened to be gorgeous sisters wearing straw hats and short skirts, picked me up. They were from Knoxville but were headed to Durham. I rode for eight hours with the sisters. It was quietly stunning.

So when the driver of the crusty minivan dropped me off at the Highway 97 junction to Sunriver, it wasn't fear or abandonment I felt, it was exhilaration. I was moving. The scenery had shifted, if only some ten miles south. I stood at that junction for 15 minutes before a beat-up, tiny red car bolted from the highway and left a trail of hazy grain in its wake of departure to the gravel pits off the paved road. As with every ride I gathered on the trip, I quickly picked my pack from the side of the road and jogged to the vehicle.

Two young men, clearly hoodlums and stinking of raw whiskey, were seated in the front seats. A highway patrolman happened to cruise by just as I was entering the dark confines of the small automobile. The cop bolted from the highway, pulling off several hundred feet in front of our vehicle. Seconds later, and immediately after we passed him, the cop zipped back to the highway and positioned himself directly behind our stunned, staggered passengers in the car.

There I was, stuck in the back of some shitty car with two burnt-out drunkards cruising south down Highway 97 with a highway patrol officer on our tail and absolutely no reason to have hope. The driver, who never told me his name, had his pale hands gripped tight to the black steering wheel. The passenger took long gulps from a McDonald's cup I can only assume contained a mixture of fountain soda and booze.

"Is he still back there?" the passenger asked about the cop. "Why's he fucking with us again?"

"Son of a bitch," the driver snapped, "always messing with the locals. Never the tourists. Just the locals."

I kept quiet, fearing the duo might suspect me to be some kind of cop informant. Fortunately, the highway patrolman took a right turn several miles later and was never seen again.

The boys were headed home to La Pine after a hard morning of what they told me was "work." When it comes to young people from La Pine, particularly those who stink of booze at 8:30 in the morning on a Tuesday, it's never clear what "work" really means. I kept my questions and conversation to a minimum and pretended to be cool.

"Yeah," I said. "I hate cops."

The statement was so cliché I'm lucky they didn't gut me on the spot. Rather, we just kept plowing south.

The La Pine boys dropped me off at the far end of town directly across the street from a Ray's Grocery Store. It was just before 9 a.m. The sun continued to heat the earth. I shed the bottom half of my pants that zip off into shorts. The flow of traffic had increased substantially. Dozens of large motor homes had boomed past, full of empty space and old couples who refused to even take a glimpse in my direction. Some truckers would wave, but in nearly an hour's time, no one had stopped.

Sometime before ten, a young woman working at a nearby espresso stand shouted out "Hey, do you want a cup of coffee?"

I did. All I'd had before leaving town that morning was some instant-coffee crap that tasted like dirty old beans. Fresh java sounded delicious. The barista, Natalie, told me she had once hitched from Coos Bay to Portland with seven of her girlfriends.

"I know what you're going through," she said. "Don't worry, you'll get there." I told Natalie I had no money to pay for the coffee.

"It's on me," she said. Her hair was a golden shade of yellow and I considered abandoning my plans and asking her to lunch. Instead, I slowly strolled back to my pack, the sign and the nearby highway. Minutes later, Darrell pulled over.

Darrell drove a big-ass semi. He's a short black man from Detroit who knew and talked nothing but baseball.

"We got a fine roster this year," Darrell explained. "Sheffield, Pudge, Verlander, we got it all."

Darrell was heading to L.A. to pick up some heavy load – he didn't know what of – and transport it to Texas.

"I'm really retired," Darrell told me. "I just bought this truck to see the country. That's all."

I enjoyed Darrell's presence and wouldn't have minded riding clear to L.A with him. The land fascinated him, and it felt safe inside that massive cab. As we neared the junction of Highway 138, which rolls past Crater Lake and directly to the Mt. Thielsen trailhead, my peak emerged in the distance.

"There's where I'm going to hike," I said, pointing in the direction of the huge mountain.

Darrell stared west, and it was like that scene in *Field of Dreams* where James Earl Jones slaps on his glasses as he and

Costner travel down the Iowa farm road to the lighted, magical baseball field.

"Well, I'll be," Darrell said. "I ain't never met anybody who ever walked a mountain like that."

It was one of the finest compliments I'd ever received. Soon after, Darrell dropped me off at the junction to the westbound highway, and we parted ways with a handshake.

"Careful up there, son," he said. "I don't want to read about you in the papers."

"Darrell," I said. "You'll read me IN the papers."

Natalie's coffee had moved through me at a rapid rate so I scampered into a stand of pines that overlooked the highway junction and took a leak. It was just past 11 and getting amply warm outside.

Upon returning to the roadside, the first vehicle that passed pulled over to pick me up. It was a golden four-door Honda Accord, the same make and model as my own great Shark. An elderly gentleman was behind the wheel and he was traveling alone.

"Put your bags in the back," he said, his eyes hidden by a pair of dark sunglasses. "Just mind the cherries."

The old man's back seat was filled with several boxes of fresh, swollen cherries from some nearby organic farm. With grace, I slid my pack and sign upon the fruit. Then I moved to the passenger side and got in.

"My name's Gene," the driver said. "I have a medical marijuana card and I'm about to partake in some grass."

"Okay, Gene," I said. "It's your ship."

Gene was holding a finely-rolled joint that he lit almost immediately after I entered the car. He smoked the entire thing to himself during the first ten minutes of our ride together, neither mentioning it again nor offering me a drag.

"So what do you do for work?" Gene finally said, a fine, thick layer of marijuana smoke coating the inside of the vehicle.

"I'm a writer," I said.

"A writer? You got a job?"

"Sure," I said. "Three of them."

"Then how come you ain't got no wheels?"

"I do. Just felt like hitching."

"I dig it," Gene said.

Twenty miles later the old man dropped me at the trailhead. It had taken me four rides and just shy of five hours to reach my destination. Many said it couldn't, or simply shouldn't be done. But to hell with that kind of thinking and breed. That type of mindset simply won't do me any good.

I spent the next two days hiking through some of the most pristine mountain terrain I've ever explored. I saw four people just beyond the trailhead, one of whom warned me that they'd seen four bears the day before. Other than those initial folk, I saw no people or spoke to anyone during my time in the woods. I hiked seven miles to my camp at 9,000 feet. Two attempts at the Thielsen's summit left me just shy on both runs. I didn't eat much or do anything other than hike and read when I was up there. Alone. And really, I didn't want to.

I woke up at 5 a.m. the day I was due back in Bend and slugged the seven miles back down to the highway. It took two rides – one of them taking me 96 percent of the way – to get home.

I went hitchhiking and mountain climbing through the wild country of Oregon. I didn't spend one dime after walking out my front door that first morning.

And I plan to do it again.

Soon.

Publisher's Note: This story by Joseph Friedrichs originally appeared July 1, 2007 on the news site NewWest.Net.

Dock Fishing

I've never owned a fishing vessel. Not once have I said to another living soul the following statement: "Would you like to take a ride in my boat?"

The main reason for this is simple: I am a dock fisherman. I am a shoreline fisherman. I am a simple man with simple needs. And believe it or not, I'm cool with that.

For me, fishing isn't about high-tech gear and gadgets. I don't spend countless hours and wads of money to outwit the fish on which I prey. My tactics are simple and rarely call for anything more than a rod, a reel, a pole and live bait. Maybe, just maybe, I'll use a lure or some type of fly when opting to get fancy.

To be honest, I loathe the tech-saturated fishermen of the world. Those dudes – it's always grown men – who think they're on the Bassmaster Tour even though they're fishing a 2-acre pond with a maximum depth of 10 feet. These are the same guys who wear $300 polarized sunglasses and always have a ball cap on. A camouflage hat, typically.

To me, the best part of fishing is being outside and taking on a challenge. Using gadgets and gizmos seems counterintuitive. Having a machine locate all the fish you seek does not interest me. In fact, it disturbs me. Allowing for good luck and intuition to find the fish is my style. Always has been. Always will be.

Recently I was fishing a small body of water in north-central Minnesota known as Echo Lake. It's a quaint body of water, about 5 acres in size. Just my style. Branching out of my usual standards of fishing from the shore, or at best a manmade dock, I rented a kayak/canoe hybrid from the nearby ranger station inside the state park where Echo Lake sits.

The water was calm on the lake as I ventured from the eastern shoreline to a nearby peninsula. My rented watercraft was not the only vessel on Echo Lake that afternoon. In fact, there were dozens of fishing boats scattered across the water. All about there were silver and gold boats with names like Lund, Alumacraft and Pond King emblazoned on their sides. The aforementioned fishermen types wearing expensive sunglasses and cammo hats were sitting on swivel-style chairs on the boats. Nobody seemed to be smiling for some reason.

Meanwhile, I paddled about gently and found myself whistling a jolly tune for no reason other than the fact the sun was out and my life was damn good. Fish or no fish, luck or no luck, I enjoy being outdoors and testing the odds. This act of fishing was supposed to be enjoyable. Isn't that why we went?

Now for some reason, and I'm not entirely sure why, I decided it didn't matter if I caught any fish that particular afternoon. Instead, my mission was to disturb, annoy and get under the skin of any fisherman in a motorized boat.

And so I did.

My adventure started on the tip of the peninsula, about 30 yards from the northeast shoreline. Two men in a sparkling-blue Lund boat were casting crankbaits like goons. Neither of the men appeared to be enjoying themselves. Their art seemed to be some sort of labor. One man had a disgusting brown mustache. The other had the appearance of true degeneracy.

"Howdy, gentlemen!" I said loudly as I approached their boat.

One of them did a sort of half-wave and clearly seemed annoyed at my enthusiasm.

"Fish ain't biting today but the sun is cooking me like a Thanksgiving turkey!" I said, again speaking very loudly.

Both men took another cast and ignored my comment.

I paddled closer and continued my rant.

"I wouldn't cast over there if I were you," I said to the men, "fish haven't been swimming in those parts since Old Man Peabody dumped that drum of oil right where you just cast that lure. Nope, only thing you'll catch down there is a mutated frog."

I started to laugh manically and paddled off.

My next target was a father-and-son combo. The father puffed on a Marlboro cigarette. The son spit in the water every few seconds like a moronic ballplayer stuck in the minors. They too were fishing from a Lund. For bait they were using green jigs with a minnow attached. The father was probably 50 and the son 20.

"Do you guys have any beer I could buy from you?" I asked while approaching their boat.

The father shook his head no. The son laughed quietly, seemingly embarrassed.

"I am thirsty as a horse and my woman's got me dry on the sauce," I said. "I haven't been this thirsty for a drink in years. I would go back to my days as an alter boy with that touchy-feely priest if I could land some of that church wine right now."

I belted out with crazed laughter. Then I continued.

"You fellers know where the strip joint is around here? I got a hankering for some nasty-old poontang."

The father started the boat's motor and sped away without saying a word.

After that I paddled to a group of two boats fishing a reef near the middle of the lake. There were three men in one boat and two in the other. They appeared not to know one another. I placed my kayak in between the two parties. After tying on my heaviest jig I let my line drop to the bottom. I bounced and moved the jig until it was snared on something below. A classic snag. This was precisely my plan. When I was certain the hook was set on the bottom and would not budge, I began shouting and making a tremendous scene.

"Holy sweet Jesus!" I roared. "I got the big one! I finally got the legend! I got him boys!"

All five of the fishermen nearby immediately became fascinated and some reeled in their lines in order to make room. My antics continued.

"He's a monster! He is pulling so hard my arm might break! Help me God! Oh somebody help me!"

All the while my rod was bent nearly in half. The line screamed from the tension of the log, or boulder, or whatever had my jig snagged at the bottom of the lake.

"Mother of Moses, I got the biggest fish in the whole damn state!"

After 30 seconds of this madness the other fishermen realized I was lying. And yet, I continued.

"It's running deep again, boys! Clear the way! This hog is going to battle me until sundown!"

Nobody said a word, but both engines came to life from the nearby boats. They started to drive away.

"Call the preacher!" I screamed.

Well, there it was. I had what I consider one of my most enjoyable fishing experiences ever. My stringer was empty and that night for dinner I ate the best hamburger I've had in 15 years. After that I slept like a king knowing the fishermen with motorized boats were awake, wondering why their lives weren't going exactly as they planned.

Four Corners

Down in the canyon lands, near the Four-Corners area where Colorado, Utah, New Mexico and Arizona come together, lives a man who quit using guns.

It was an unexpected and sudden choice by the man. After all, he'd been hunting his entire adult life. In his home he had a gun cabinet containing an assortment of 18 rifles, handguns and shotguns. And nearly everywhere the man went he carried a pistol on his hip.

Then one day, he gave all 18 guns to his neighbor.

"Take these," the man said. Then he walked away.

The choice to quit using and likewise owning guns wasn't political. This man, who went by the name of Daniel, did so because he was tired of thinking about death.

And really, that's what a gun is: a weapon used to end something. Either a life, or a tin can, or whatever it is somebody is shooting at.

So instead of shooting and carrying a gun, Daniel started walking.

He hiked the Dry Wash Trail in the Manti-La National forest on the north side of Blanding in southeast Utah. The forest there is a mix of Ponderosa Pines and Douglas Firs, Aspens, Maples, Narrowleaf Cottonwoods and Gambel Oak.

Daniel thought to himself that the area would be prime for hunting jackrabbits, and in the fall for mule deer. Old ways of thinking die hard, Daniel discovered.

This being his first hike in more than 40 years without carrying a gun, Daniel realized those type of notions no longer mattered. What was important now was exploring Earth, seeing how it made him feel to be alive, touching the rocks and smelling the air.

It made him feel good, Daniel decided.

After his first journey, Daniel proceeded to hike the entire 51.7 mile Grand Gulch Primitive Area Trail in the Cedar Mesa area, also located in southeast Utah. In this region Daniel came across dozens of pictographs, ruins and a whole galaxy of riparian habitat along the canyon floor. Pinon Pine, Utah Juniper and other desert vegetation were scattered along the canyon sides of the trail. Never in his life had Daniel paid such close attention to his natural surroundings. Before he dropped the gun, all he noticed were places an animal might be hiding. Now, without a mission to kill in his forethoughts, Daniel could be completely aware of his environment.

This made him feel good, Daniel decided.

Leaving Utah, Daniel made his way east. It was there he hiked the Blue Lakes Trail, which guided him 3.3 miles to Lower Blue Lake in the Sneffels Wilderness of the

Uncompahgre National Forest in southwest Colorado. On this journey Daniel was surrounded by 12,000 ft. mountain peaks and sweet-smelling pines.

Near the 2-mile mark of his hike, Daniel came across a large bull elk grazing in a meadow. The elk's antlers branched from its head like magnificent limbs from some mobile tree. The body of the animal was muscular and rippled with each movement. Daniel paused when he located the elk, careful not to send waves of fear in its direction. For 25 seconds the two stood, calmly and intently staring at one another. His previous thought pattern would certainly have involved killing the animal, but now Daniel wanted nothing more than to share the meadow and the moment with the elk. And so he did.

This made him feel good, Daniel decided.

After several days of camping, meditation and utter bliss at Lower Blue Lake, Daniel ventured to New Mexico. His destination was the Narrows Rim Trail, a 7.8 mile round-trip hike along the mesa top overlooking the Narrows area of El Malpais, located in the far northwest reaches of the state.

For some reason, prior to his departure, Daniel felt he should carry a pistol with him on the hike. He quickly dismissed the sentiment, remembering the good feelings brought on by his recent adventures into the wilderness without carrying a weapon. A backslide into his old ways would be destructive to the serenity he presently felt. Progress, Daniel realized, was why he wanted to walk without carrying a weapon.

Near the junction of the trail where the path splits and begins the loop home, Daniel felt he was being watched. The hair on his neck stood on end. His sense of security dwindled. Something was stalking Daniel. All his years in the wild brought this realization quickly and without question. And indeed Daniel's instincts were correct. A mountain lion was following him.

Daniel cursed quietly, wishing he'd brought the pistol. Now he was unarmed, being stalked by a killer cat and had few options other than to hope and pray. And so he did. Standing on a nearby rock, about the size of a pickup truck, Daniel started to pray out loud. Raised without religion, Daniel didn't understand who he was praying to, what God was, or where his thoughts were going. He just prayed.

This made him feel good, Daniel decided.

During his prayers, Daniel didn't make any special requests. He did not ask for the lion to go away, to be killed, or any such demands. All he asked for was continued serenity in that moment – a chance to accept what was reality. During the course of his prayers, Daniel watched the mountain lion as it scurried across the mesa, bouncing from ledge to ledge with ease and grace. It was a beautiful animal, Daniel decided. And it was home, there in the forest, where it knew nothing but to survive. Had Daniel been carrying the gun, he would have shot the cougar. He would have done so without mercy the instant their eyes locked for that briefest of moments. Instead, he continued to pray.

Not long after, the mountain lion wandered off. It was not interested in eating, nor even so much as harming Daniel. The cat only wanted to investigate this human form as it moved through the high desert. The cat had every reason to be in that national forest. So did Daniel. There was absolutely no reason to go killing every potential predator simply because he felt threatened. There is a harmony to nature. The gun is an unnatural disrupter to this balance, to this harmony Daniel now understood for the first time.

This made him feel good, Daniel decided.

After stopping for gas in Shiprock, New Mexico, Daniel continued west where he planned to hike the Little Ruins Trail in northeast Arizona. The sun was shining and Daniel felt more at peace with nature than at any previous moment in his life. There were no automobiles in the parking lot at the trailhead, so Daniel was correct when he assumed nobody else was on the hiking trail that afternoon. It was his path to explore in complete solitude.

About three-fourths of a mile down the Little Ruins Trail, a 60-inch Western Diamond-backed Rattlesnake bit Daniel in the leg. The snake was fierce, literally launching from the brush to plunge its fangs and venom into Daniel.

Writhing there on the tail, with bits of white foam and spittle shooting from his mouth, Daniel had visions of waterfalls and emerald-colored pools along a pristine river. He was alone and near comatose, his body suffering from serious necrosis. Daniel thought of all the animals he'd killed with a gun. He remembered the elk he dropped with German-designed Sauer 303 rifle. He blew the elk's inside from it's chest cavity at a distance of 20 yards. He remembered the glory he felt when he killed an animal, regardless of his reason in doing so. Daniel was a hunter. He could kill animals with a gun.

This made him feel good, Daniel decided.

Trout Country Wandering

I spent the summer of 2004 on a large ranch in the Boulder Valley of Montana, located about 20 miles from Helena, as the crow flies. My official title that summer was "intern" at the local newspaper, but really I was a full-time fisherman. I took my job very seriously. On a side note, it wasn't all that bad working at the newspaper either.

The ranch where I lived was, and forever shall be known as the Carey Ranch. The chances of corporate greed or sterilized shopping malls arriving to the Boulder Valley are essentially, and hopefully, zero percent. The Ranch encompasses more than 85,000 acres of land, most of it used for grazing livestock. The Carey family has been on this land for several generations, tracing back to the early 1900s. These are cowboys, ranchers and hard-working men and women. They were the real-deal too, not like some sucker over in Bozeman or Missoula driving a Dodge pickup because he thinks it makes him cool and "Montana-ish." The Carey family, to me, is the Boulder Valley. They are the roots of Montana.

When I arrived to the valley that summer from the University of Montana, some 150 miles to the southwest in Missoula, I didn't know what to expect. I was prone to nightlife, earning my money as a bartender and chasing girls as though it were a requirement of existence. On The Ranch there would be none of that. It was the Careys and me. In charge of the operations were Tom and Helen, both of whom were in their late 60s. Their sons, Tommy and Chris, orchestrated most of the general labor, but it was still Tom and Helen who sat atop the hierarchy of the Ranch.

That summer, the nearest bar was more than 10 miles from where I lived. The closest girl without a wedding ring on her finger was probably double that distance. I had two choices that summer: Go mad from isolation, or embrace the solitude and take every opportunity I had to go fishing. I chose the latter. It was the wisest move I've ever made.

My arrival to the Boulder Valley came at the conclusion of a vicious run of heavy drinking. It was the of spring term at the University of Montana, and liquor went hand-in-hand with my journalism classmates and our future plans.

"I'll be working this summer in Washington, chasing politicians and lobbyists for quotes all day and night," one particularly sinister classmate of mine said toward the end of the semester. What else is there to say to someone like that, other than to nod and take a large pull directly from a bottle of bourbon?

While my colleagues followed the big-city lights for

their internships, I steered my ship to one of Montana's most beautiful and remote valleys. Cut only by the sparsely-traveled Highway 69, my temporary home was located literally within a stone's throw from the Boulder River, a low-flowing tributary of the Jefferson River. Trout, some of them living a portion of their lives without ever being harassed by a fisherman, swam freely in the waters I viewed all summer from the window in my room. What the river lacked in size it compensated for in trout per square mile. The untapped potential for fishing was amazing. I knew it. The Careys probably knew it too. The only difference was they didn't give a lick about fishing. Private property for fishing is a great thing in the West. Leaving the bars and college life behind seemed strange to some of my friends, but isolation is a gift when used properly.

The Ranch sits at just under 5,000 feet. When I first pulled my 1995 Honda Accord into the long gravel driveway, it started to snow. The date was June 7. I thought about weeping and driving back to Missoula for a beer with the boys.

"Yes fellas, it was snowing when I got there so I said screw it and came on home. Let's get crazy!" I romanticized in my head.

Instead, I went inside and had a cup of coffee with Tom

and Helen Carey.

"You can fish wherever you want on our land," Helen said cheerfully. "Just make yourself at home."

I will always remember that moment, as few words are more welcome to a fisherman.

Not long after we finished our coffee, Tom disappeared out the back door. I saw him drive off to the fields on a 4-wheeler equipped with shovels, rakes and a small rifle. Helen too made her way outside, but not before she changed into boots and put on a some leather gloves. Not leather in the New York City kind of way, but rather in that rough, yellow, sturdy-Montana style.

The snow had quit falling and the sun came blasting through a series of white, non-threatening clouds. The valley was exposed and a golden hue took to the terrain. Snow-covered peaks showcased the Tobacco Root Mountains, some 45 miles to the southeast. I took a deep breath and realized I was home. It was time to start fishing.

For the record, I am not a master fly fisherman. My capacity in the field of fly fishing remains, and shall forever remain a work in progress. As I approached for the first time the narrow stretch of the Boulder River near The Ranch, I realized fly fishing was going to be extremely challenging. All matter of shrubs, heavy brush and vine-like plants spanned the shoreline. To make things less complicated, I took my spinning rod and tied on a silver and yellow Panther Martin lure. At least I wouldn't have to deal with a precise back-cast necessary in fly fishing, I reasoned.

Walking with some hesitation, I veered through an open fence into a cattle pen. The ground was covered with dried (choose the four-letter word you like best, dear reader) and I followed what appeared to be a faint trail up river. About 300 yards later, I discovered what would become my favorite fishing hole of the summer. The hole formed between two curves in the river, a type of oxbow pool deep enough to hold fish even through the hottest stretches of the summer. Looking around to make sure nobody was eyeing my fishing tactics, I stepped forward and made my first cast of the summer. With the grace of an eagle, my spinner flew into the waiting arms of a thorny bush on the opposite bank.

"What the...?" I said aloud.

After much wrenching, pulling and twisting, the lure came free. It landed just off the bank, on the edges of the pool. What appeared to be a doomed cast instantly morphed into excellence. A few simple cranks of the reel later, and something damn-near pulled the entire rod from my grip. That something turned out to be my first trout of the summer. It was the most beautiful brown trout I'd ever seen, 18-inches of golden creation so stunning I had to sit down right there on the rocky banks of the Boulder River.

For the next three months, I could count on that hole, just a few minutes walk from my summer home, to produce fish. I found many more places to fish along the river, but none were as deep and reliable as that first hole. When I made boastful proclamations to staff or visitors in the newspaper office about my fishing fortunes, I could always back that up the next day by bringing them a fish from that hole.

"Plenty more where that came from," I would say, handing them a perfectly-cleaned and gutted 20-inch trout sealed tightly in a Ziploc bag. "You might want to keep that on ice until dinner."

Then I would wink and walk away while whistling a coy little tune.

There are different roads, means and styles of having a good time. This was my prime discovery during my summer on The Ranch. It's easy to get lost in the drama and rawness of nightlife, regardless of the population or location where it takes place. What can be more of a challenge is finding peace and accepting the slowness of life alone on an 85,000 acre ranch. The Careys work harder than any collective group I've known, using every hour of daylight as though it were a gift. My only real task was to stay out of trouble, write a few stories and fish. For me, it opened that door into pure living. I didn't need mass substances to alter my perception. I saw the amount of joy that simply being on The Ranch brought to the Careys. The simple life brought simple pleasures: seeing the sun dip below the mountains, watching a crane stalk through a marsh, listening to the horses in the morning, not hearing automobiles for an entire day.

While the fishing was reliable and filled many hours of my time, a highlight of the summer came during what was scheduled to be a relaxing afternoon hike through the nearby Boulder Mountains. Helen dropped me off at a hunting cabin the Carey family owns, located about 10 miles from The Ranch. The hike was indeed relaxing, until I crossed paths with the bear.

Descending from a steep ridge and following a path back to the cabin, I noticed a small creature moving in the woods to my right. Having seen dozens of the Carey's cattle in the hills that afternoon, the movement didn't stir much of a reaction in my senses. It wasn't until I noticed the mother bear, standing about 40 yards away and to my left that fear struck.

Not only was I know in the proximity of a mother bear and her cub, but I was directly between them. According to the strict laws of nature, this was a definite error. It was strange, I remember thinking, I've had such great luck fishing all summer, and now the exact opposite fortune finds me while walking alone in bear country. Mother Nature, it seems, has no favorite child.

"Sweet Jesus," I muttered when I realized the seriousness of the situation.

Truth be told, I was well educated about reacting to bear encounters. One thing I knew for sure was that running provokes a bear. I should not run, I thought. And then, without any hesitation whatsoever, I took off in a dead sprint.

I never won any medals on the track team in school. I don't consider myself a fine sprinter. On this day, however, I ran faster than anyone in Montana had during the past 15 years. Without once stopping to look back and see if the bear gave chase, I ran toward the cabin. It was a downhill jaunt, covering about 800 yards from the spot where I first saw the bear. For all I know, the bear was on my heels the whole way and I somehow managed to outrun the beast. As I said, I never looked back.

It's worth noting that during my hike that afternoon I happened to be carrying the very expensive digital camera that belonged to the newspaper where I was completing my internship. The camera was worth at least $1,000. My life was valuable, at least to some, but when I made it back to the cabin after successfully fleeing from the bears, I noticed the camera was no longer dangling around my neck. Somehow, during the commotion, it had been left behind.

There are moments in life when men and women have to make very important decisions. Life decisions, we'll call them. Safely situated there at the cabin, gathering my breath from the sudden and unexpected burst of unwanted exercise, I faced one of these life decisions. Should I go back for the camera? Or should I say it was used in self defense against the bear and probably saved my life?

After a few moments spent gathering my senses, I opted to head back up the mountain and reclaim the camera. Why? Because I didn't want to lose my internship, and I most certainly didn't want to lose anything because of a damn bear. That's why.

Slowly walking back to the scene of the encounter, I took caution in every step. The wind picked up, making it difficult to hear anything other than my most immediate surroundings. And then, without any warning, something burst from the nearby bushes.

I take a certain pride in my manhood. It's nothing more than primitive male behavior at work, but nonetheless, I enjoy who I am and represent as a male human being. That's why it comes with a certain degree of difficulty to admit that the sound I made when the animal I am about to mention came charging out from the bushes, about 2-feet in front of me, was a sound so high-pitched that most teenage girls would be unable to match its shrillness.

The sound went something like this: "Eeeeehhhhhheeeeeee!!!!"

My hands covered my face while I squealed. My body trembled. Life, it seemed, was coming to an end.

And then I looked down and saw the chipmunk standing there. It was tiny, even by chipmunk standards. Nothing more had come crashing from the brush other than this little creature. My nerves were so on edge prior to that, all I could do was laugh out loud and keep walking up the mountain.

About 700 yards later, I saw my camera sitting on the side of the trail. At some point, though I have no recollection of this, I must have decided to take a picture of the bear. Before I could, the bear's activity must have scared me into the unconscious state that sent me flailing down the mountain. Anyhow, I never saw the bear again.

During the course of my summer spent on The Ranch, the Carey family had me tell what forever became known as "The Bear Story" at least two-dozen times. Each time they would laugh and laugh, enjoying the innocence (and perhaps luck and stupidity) of a city boy wandering the mountains. Regardless of why they enjoyed the story, it was ours to share.

It was The Ranch that taught me the excellence of life in the country, particularly in mountain valleys still untouched by modern civilization and development. There is excellence in that bear story, simply because it is true and the power involved with imagining all the various outcomes. What if that bear had chased me down the mountain? What if it had been a mountain lion that came crashing out of the brush, instead of a chipmunk? The Ranch is full of great stories where you don't need cheap liquor to capture the punch line. The Ranch is real. The Boulder Valley is real. When you're out there, everything else seems petty.

During the summer of 2004, I spent more than half my time fishing. The remainder of my hours awake were spent hiking through the mountains or scribbling stories in a Montana newsroom. I didn't have a girlfriend. I didn't have much money. I ate a ton of fresh trout.

It was the best summer of my life.

ABOUT THE AUTHOR

Joseph Friedrichs is an author, poet and journalist. He attended the University of Montana, studying journalism and fishing.

His writing has been featured in *The New York Times* and dozens of other publications. In 2005 he was awarded the Robert F. Kennedy Award for excellence in journalism.

His first book, *Down Like Lazarus*, was published in 2011.

www.ingramcontent.com/pod-product-compliance
Lightning Source LLC
Chambersburg PA
CBHW060642290526
45793CB00001B/364